She liked to graze in the fields and munch the sweet hay.

3

Each year, the alpacas had a Sports Day.

When Sports Day started, Iris liked to hide.

You lot make me feel tired!

5

"Run with us, Iris!" said her friend, Miles.
"You might win a prize!"

6

But Iris stayed away from the starting line.

The rest of the alpacas started lining up.

Iris sat in the shade. But then she felt a sharp bite!

The insect bite felt like fire! Iris jumped, but the insect did not slide off.

Iris did a wild jump. She banged into the tree and ...

11

... the farm cat landed SPLAT on Iris's back!

Iris sprinted down the field. She jumped across the stile, into the farmer's garden.

Yikes!

The farmer's wet socks and vests were on the line.

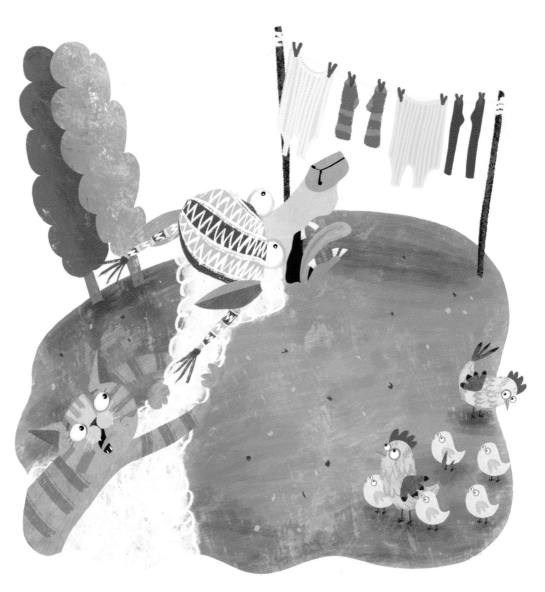

Crash! All the wet items ended up on Iris's neck.

Iris jumped across the gate and started sliding down the lane.

There was LOTS of mud and slime!
Iris and the cat went quicker and quicker.

They went gliding down to the end of the lane. Iris did a final jump, back into the field.

Iris's friends had started to run.

A wild monster!

Iris sprinted down the field, and across the finishing line!

"Iris!" smiled Miles. "You get the prize!"
The cat got a prize too!

Iris's wild ride

22

23

After reading

Letters and Sounds: Phase 5

Word count: 243

Focus phonemes: /ai/ ay, ey, a-e /ee/ ie, ea /igh/ i, i-e

Common exception words: the, to, she, when, me, you, all, there, was, said, friend, into, were, do, of

Curriculum links: Science: Animals, including humans; Physical Education

National Curriculum learning objectives: Reading/word reading: read accurately by blending sounds in unfamiliar words containing GPCs that have been taught; read words containing taught GPCs and -s, -es, -ing, -ed, -er and -est endings; Reading/comprehension: understand both the books they can already read accurately and fluently and those they listen to by checking that the text makes sense to them as they read, and correcting inaccurate reading

Developing fluency

- Your child may enjoy hearing you read the book.
- Take turns to read a double page, including any speech bubbles. Check that your child pauses for ellipses to build the suspense.

Phonic practice

- Challenge your child to find words in the story with -ing and -ed endings and to read them aloud:

  -ing (e.g. page 7 *starting*, page 8 *lining*, page 16 *sliding*, page 18 *gliding*, page 20 *finishing*)

  -ed (e.g. page 5 *started*, *tired*, page 7 *stayed*, page 13 *sprinted*, page 15 *ended*)
- Look together at page 15. Ask your child to find words with the /igh/ sound. (*items, Iris's, like*) Ask them to read them aloud.

Extending vocabulary

- Look at pages 2 and 3 and find the word **sweet** on both pages. Ask your child to think of another word with a similar meaning for each. (e.g. page 2: *pleasant, lovely*; page 3: *tasty, sugary*)
- Look at pages 10 and 11 and ask your child to think of another word with a similar meaning for each of the following:

  jumped (e.g. *bounded, leapt*)   banged (e.g. *bumped, knocked*)